D1200575

DEC 2004

CONNETQUOT PUBLIC LIBRARY

0621 9100 331 819 9

$ 30·00

CONNETQUOT PUBLIC LIBRARY
760 Ocean Avenue
Bohemia, NY   11716
631-567-5079

Library Hours:

Monday - Friday	9:00 - 9:00
Saturday	9:00 - 5:00
Sunday (Oct. - May)	1:00 - 5:00

GAYLORD M

RIO DE JANEIRO

MARION MORRISON

CONNETQUOT PUBLIC LIBRARY
760 OCEAN AVENUE
BOHEMIA, NEW YORK 11716
Tel: (631) 567-5079

Please visit our web site at: www.worldalmanaclibrary.com
For a free color catalog describing World Almanac® Library's list of high-quality books
and multimedia programs, call 1-800-848-2928 (USA) or 1-800-387-3178 (Canada).
World Almanac® Library's fax: (414) 332-3567.

Library of Congress Cataloging-in-Publication Data available upon request from publisher.
Fax (414) 336-0157 for the attention of the Publishing Records Department.

ISBN 0-8368-5031-9 (lib. bdg.)
ISBN 0-8368-5191-9 (softcover)

First published in 2004 by
World Almanac® Library
330 West Olive Street, Suite 100
Milwaukee, WI 53212 USA

Copyright © 2004 by World Almanac® Library.

Produced by Discovery Books
Editor: Kate Taylor
Series designers: Laurie Shock, Keith Williams
Designer and page production: Keith Williams
Photo researcher: Rachel Tisdale
Maps and diagrams: Stefan Chabluk
World Almanac® Library editorial direction: Mark J. Sachner
World Almanac® Library editor: Jenette Donovan Guntly
World Almanac® Library art direction: Tammy Gruenewald
World Almanac® Library production: Jessica Morris

Photo credits: South American Pictures/Tony Morrison: cover and title page; Art Directors & Trip: p.4;
Art Directors & Trip/D. Harding: p.36; James Davis Photography: pp.20, 41; James Davis Worldwide: p.38;
Hutchison/Sarah Errington: p.16; Hutchison/Maurice Harvey: p.23; Hutchison/Jeremy Horner: pp.27, 31;
North Wind Picture Archives: p.10; South American Pictures: pp.8, 13, 14; South American Pictures/
Robert Francis: p.15; South American Pictures/Jason P. Howe: pp.19, 21, 25, 39; South American Pictures/
Tony Morrison: pp.12, 24, 30, 32, 33, 35, 37, 40, 43; Still Pictures/Mark Edwards: p.42; Still Pictures/
John Maier: pp.22, 29

Cover caption: Rio's famous landmark, Sugarloaf Mountain, can be seen across Botafogo Bay.

All rights reserved. No part of this book may be reproduced, stored in a retrieval system, or transmitted in any form or
by any means, electronic, mechanical, photocopying, recording, or otherwise, without the prior written permission of
the copyright holder.

Printed in the United States of America

1 2 3 4 5 6 7 8 9 08 07 06 05 04

Contents

Introduction

Rio de Janeiro, in Brazil, is one of the world's most spectacular cities. It extends along a ribbon of hilly land between the calm, dark blue waters of the bay and a backdrop of lush, forested hills and rocky peaks.

Christ the Redeemer
On Corcovado (Hunchback) Mountain, which stands 2,310 feet (704 meters) high, towers a 98-foot (30-m) tall statue of Christ the Redeemer, arms outstretched in welcome or, some say, in divine forgiveness.

◄ Copacabana, one of the most famous sunbathing beaches in the world, is also used for outdoor concerts with temporary stands and dressing rooms.

Carioca

When the Portuguese first arrived in Guanabara Bay, one of the first things they built was a stone house beside a small river. The Tamoio (Native peoples) called it Carioca, or "house of the white man." The river by which it sat came to be known by the same name, and eventually, so did the people of Rio.

Sugarloaf Mountain

Small islands and outcroppings of rock litter Guanabara Bay. The most famous is the Pão de Açúcar, or Sugarloaf Mountain, a mountain that stands 1,296 feet (395 m) tall. It gets its name from its shape, which is similar to the cone used in the process of converting sugarcane into sugar.

"From the top [of Sugarloaf] I had my first panorama of Rio de Janeiro — fold upon fold of peak and rock and island like rumpled bedclothes; slopes bare and brown, or awash with blue-green vegetation; hilltops sprinkled with buildings, their roofs glittering in the sun; deep clefts and gullies down which houses, pink, white, and blue, straggled among the masses of foliage...."

—Gilbert Phelps, British television (BBC) producer.

CITY FACTS

Rio de Janeiro
Capital of State of Rio de Janeiro

Founded: 1565

Area (City): 487 square miles (1,261 square kilometers)

Area (Metropolitan): 16,953 square miles (43,909 sq km)

Population (City): 5,850,000

Population (Metropolitan): 14,400,000

Population Density (City): 12,012 per square mile (4,639 per sq km)

Population Density (Metropolitan): 850 per square mile (328 per sq km)

Leisure Time

The people of Rio are known as *Cariocas*. Every day, crowds of Cariocas fill Rio de Janeiro's beaches to sunbathe, chat, relax, work out, or play soccer. Soccer is a passion for Brazilians, and Rio is home to one of the world's largest soccer stadiums, the Maracanã. The city is also famous for its annual Carnival, a riotous festival full of color, music, dancing, and fabulous costumes. The Carnival's samba schools have become famous worldwide, with an average of four thousand dancers from each school participating in the yearly festival.

5

Metropolitan Rio

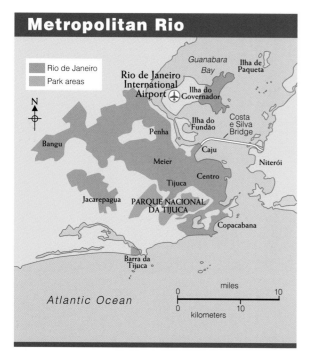

Rio de Janeiro
Park areas

N

Guanabara Bay
Ilha de Paqueta
Rio de Janeiro International Airport
Ilha do Governador
Ilha do Fundão
Costa e Silva Bridge
Penha
Caju
Niterói
Bangu
Meier
Centro
Tijuca
Jacarepagua
PARQUE NACIONAL DA TIJUCA
Copacabana
Barra da Tijuca
Atlantic Ocean

miles
0   10
0   10
kilometers

Brazil's Capital

Rio first achieved international importance because of its fine natural harbor. In the eighteenth century, it became the capital of Brazil and remained so until the new capital of Brasília was founded in 1960. Today, Rio extends far beyond its original boundaries – over 5 million people live in the city.

Marvelous City

Metropolitan Rio has both a north and south zone. Between the two is the center or "o centro," which roughly corresponds to the original historic city founded in 1565.

Rio City Center

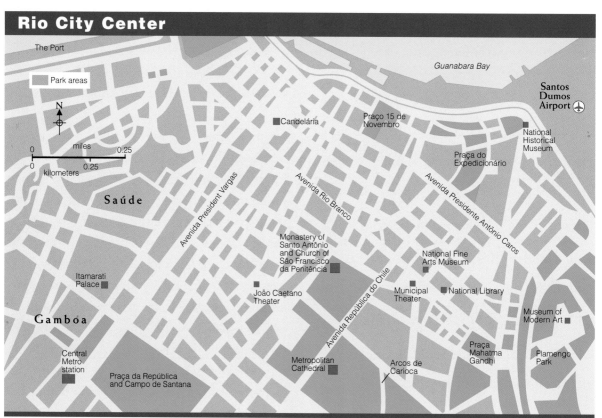

The Port

Park areas

N

miles
0   0.25
0   0.25
kilometers

Guanabara Bay

Santos Dumos Airport

Candelária
Praço 15 de Novembro
National Historical Museum
Praça do Expedicionário

Saúde

Avenida President Vargas
Avenida Rio Branco
Avenida Presidente Antônio Caros

Monastery of Santo Antônio and Church of São Francisco da Penitência
National Fine Arts Museum

Itamarati Palace

João Caetano Theater
Avenida República do Chile
Municipal Theater
National Library

Gamboa

Museum of Modern Art

Central Metro station

Praça da República and Campo de Santana

Metropolitan Cathedral
Arcos de Carioca
Praça Mahatma Gandhi
Flamengo Park

The Center

The center is now a mixture of old and new buildings. A few churches and convents remain from the colonial seventeenth and eighteenth centuries, as well as some palaces and mansions built by the Portuguese in the nineteenth century. During the same period, wide, tree-lined avenues replaced small, winding streets. In more modern times, Brazilian architects have designed ultramodern glass and concrete high-rise buildings, where much of the city's financial and commercial business is conducted today.

South Zone

The south zone developed with the opening of tunnels in 1892 and 1904 through the hills of the Serra do Mar, which had previously separated the south zone area from the city center. Wealthier families, attracted by the beaches and valleys, built houses there.

The Climate

Rio has a tropical climate tempered by cool winds from the Atlantic Ocean. The coolest months are June to August, with an average temperature of 68° Fahrenheit (20° Celsius). The hottest months are December to March, when temperatures can rise to 108° F (42° C). The rainy season lasts from October to March, and the annual rainfall is about 43 inches (110 centimeters). Rio sometimes has heavy tropical storms that cause serious flooding.

"Cidade maravilhosa" [Marvelous City]: "Wonderful city of a thousand charms, wonderful city, heart of Brazil."

—A popular old Carnival song transformed into a Carioca anthem

Many of the houses were used for weekend or holiday homes, but after about 1950, many high-rise apartment buildings were built, providing permanent homes for the less wealthy. Improved transportation has led to development farther down the coast.

North Zone

The north zone, which includes areas such as Villa Isabel and Grajau, is a mix of working and middle-class neighborhoods. Throughout the city of Rio, the hills are covered with *favelas*, or shantytowns, where millions of poor people live.

Metropolitan Area

Metropolitan Rio extends 12 miles (19 kilometers) north and more than 30 miles (48 km) west from the center. In the far north, five towns comprise the *Baixada*, or Lowland. Once small rural areas, the towns are now centers of large industrial plants and oil refineries. To the west, previously remote and untouched coastal villages are being developed into beach resorts. On the eastern shore of Guanabara Bay is the town of Niterói, a residential suburb and part of the municipality of metropolitan Rio.

CHAPTER 1

History of Rio

January River

Before the arrival of Europeans, the Rio area was populated by the Tupi-speaking Tamoio and Tememinó Native Americans. They lived simply, fishing and hunting game in the forests and wearing only colorful headdresses made from parrot and macaw feathers. The forest provided palm thatch and wood for housing, and the Native people cleared areas to grow cassava, which is also called manioc, a tropical plant with edible roots, and other crops.

On January 1, 1502, Portuguese explorers arrived in Guanabara Bay. Mistaking the bay for the mouth of a large river, they named it Rio de Janeiro or "January River." After building a small settlement, they moved to the northeast, leaving behind some Portuguese convicts, most of whom were killed by local Native people. The Portuguese explorers then settled around Salvador, on the eastern coast, where they pursued their interest in the sugar industry. The first governor-general from Portugal arrived in 1549, and in the same year, Salvador was formally founded and became the capital of the Portuguese colony of Brazil. Portuguese is still the official language spoken throughout the country.

◀ *A Dutch ship moves in to attack the port of Rio, shown in part of this seventeenth-century map.*

Meanwhile, French and Dutch traders moved in. Their business was exporting brazilwood, the wood that the country was named for. Brazilwood was highly valued in Europe for the red dye it yielded. In 1555, a party of French settlers, led by Nicholas Durand de Villegagnon, made its base on an island at the entrance of Guanabara Bay. They built a fort and called the island colony Antarctic France.

Mem de Sá

In 1560, Mem de Sá, the Portuguese governor based in Salvador, led a mission against the French. Villegagnon's colony was difficult to attack. The island had cliffs that fell straight into the ocean, and the French had the support of the local Tamoio people. The Portuguese finally captured the fort but could not stop the French from trading brazilwood. In 1565, Mem de Sá's nephew, Estácio de Sá, arrived with more ships from Portugal. He made his camp on a small beach near Sugarloaf Mountain and dedicated it to Dom Sebastião, the infant king of Portugal.

On January 20, 1567, Mem de Sá arrived from Salvador with more reinforcements, and the French were finally expelled from Brazil. During the battle, Estácio de Sá was shot by a poison arrow and died. His uncle took control and moved the Portuguese settlement to Morro do Castelo, a hill on the shore of Guanabara Bay. *São Sebastião de Rio de Janeiro* (City of Saint Sebastian of Rio de Janeiro) was founded in 1567. It is still

"I chose a site [for São Sebastião de Rio de Janeiro]… that was a great dense forest, full of many thick trees. It involved quite a lot of work cutting them down and clearing the site and building a large city… I ordered many settlers… to come and people the said city."

—From *Documentos Relativos*, by sixteenth-century Portuguese Governor Mem de Sá

the city's official name, and January 20 is a public holiday in honor of São Sebastião.

The Tamoio and Tememinó

The Tamoio and Tememinó people were enemies and took different sides when the Europeans arrived. The Tamoio supported the French, and even after their allies were defeated, the Tamoio continued to harass the Portuguese. Eventually, they were either killed or forced to flee, and by the end of the century, both Native groups had virtually disappeared.

Colonial Rio

The Morro do Castelo soon proved too cramped for the growing population. Because the local Native people were no longer a threat, settlement gradually moved down to the shore, where the beach became the main street, and canoes could be tied up right outside their owners' houses. The early settlers faced a formidable task, clearing the

▲ This eighteenth-century woodcut shows the old harbor of Rio de Janeiro when it was a Portuguese colony.

land of forest and swamps, but by the beginning of the seventeenth century, Rio had grown into a sizable town situated between four hills.

The town expanded without plans or designs. Houses and alleyways were built when and where they were needed. The wood and mud houses were low and dark, with no glass in the windows and few furnishings. The Cariocas lived on fish, whales harpooned in the bay, and cassava, a staple food for the local Native people. The town was frequently flooded, and the alleyways served as channels for the heavy rains. People made a living by fishing and trading brazilwood and sugarcane. Many churches, convents, and monasteries were built. The oldest surviving church, dating from 1624, is Nossa Senhora do Cabeça.

A Mixed Population

In 1600, Rio's population was made up of about 750 whites and 3,000 Native Americans, black African slaves, and people of mixed heritage. The male Portuguese settlers had arrived without wives and often married the Native Americans or their slaves. The resulting mixed population is the basis of society in Brazil today.

Industry

During the seventeenth century, Rio became an important port. When the sugar

Carioca Aqueduct

The main source of fresh water in Rio used to be the small Carioca River. Slaves would carry the water in buckets on their heads to the households in town, but they could barely keep up with the demand. City planners resolved the problem, though it took many years, by tapping the headwaters of the river and bringing the water into Rio by way of a magnificent aqueduct, which was 886 feet (270 m) long and, in places, 210 feet (64 m) high. The aqueduct, known as the Arcos de Carioca, was completed in 1750 and has a double row of forty-two arches. A century later, tracks were laid across the top of the aqueduct for electric streetcars. The impressive construction is still standing today.

industry around Salvador was threatened by Dutch attacks, large sugar estates and sugar mills developed farther south, and much of the sugar was exported through Rio. The city's prosperity continued with the discovery of gold and minerals in Minas Gerais, meaning "general mines," a state in the interior of Brazil. A road was constructed, linking the mines to Rio. Further prosperity was derived from a new coffee industry after plants were introduced into the Tijuca Mountains, on the southwest side of the city, in 1760. Rio replaced Salvador as the capital of Brazil in 1763 and the viceroys, officials appointed by the Portuguese royal family to govern the colony, moved to the new capital. By this time, stone houses with balconies and tiled roofs had replaced the wood and mud houses. There were gardens, public walking paths, squares, and many new churches.

The Empire

In 1807, French leader Napoleon Bonaparte threatened to depose the Portuguese monarchy. The Prince Regent, Dom João, left Portugal and, along with ten thousand courtiers, sailed to Brazil. After Napoleon's defeat in 1815, Dom João decided to stay in Brazil and took the title of King João IV of Brazil and Portugal. Conditions in Rio had improved greatly under the viceroys, but during the nineteenth century, the city was truly transformed.

Dom João encouraged greater international trade in Rio. British trading ships were among the first to arrive with manufactured goods and food products the likes of which the people of Rio had never seen. French traders came, too, eager to promote the finer things in life, such as fashions and wines.

The Cariocas could afford such things because the local coffee industry, started in the 1760s, brought prosperity to the city. Soon, Rio had its first medical school, theater, museum, printing press, newspaper, and library. For the first time, the streets were paved, lit, and policed. In 1821, Dom João returned to Portugal and left his son, Pedro, as regent to rule Brazil in his absence. The Portuguese wanted to keep Brazil as a

The Botanical Gardens

Dom João founded the Botanical Gardens in Rio in 1808. The gardens feature more than 7,000 species of tropical plants and boast 140 species of birds. Among the plants is the brazilwood tree, which is now endangered. Most spectacular are the long avenues of royal palms (below) standing some 100 feet (30 m) high.

▲ *This stately avenue of royal palms, planted in 1842, is the central feature of the Rio de Janeiro Botanical Gardens.*

colony, but Dom Pedro had other ideas. On September 7, 1822, he proclaimed Brazil's independence and made himself the country's emperor. He remained in power until 1831 when he abdicated in favor of his son, Dom Pedro II.

City Expansion

Within a few years of Dom Pedro II becoming emperor, Rio had its first steam locomotive and mule-drawn streetcars. Suburbs to the north and west grew as transportation improved. The population expanded rapidly as immigrants arrived from Europe and other parts of Brazil and as large numbers of slaves were brought in to work on the nearby coffee plantations.

For many years, the prosperous owners of the plantations lived in elegant mansions in Rio, but their lifestyle was threatened in the mid-nineteenth century when slavery began to be abolished in other parts of the world. Dom Pedro II was against slavery but was unwilling to oppose the plantation owners. In 1888, the parliament passed the so-called "Golden Law," freeing all slaves. With Dom Pedro II abroad, the bill was signed by his daughter, Princess Isabel. However, this brave act lost the royal family the support of the wealthy and powerful. In 1889, they were banished from Brazil.

Modern Republic

With the departure of the royal family, Brazil became a republic governed by civilian and military presidents. The early days of the republic coincided with the beginnings of industrialization. People began to leave the countryside to look for work in the towns and cities. Vast numbers of migrants from neighboring states settled in Rio.

Pressure on the city to expand and modernize was immense. Between 1900 and 1910, most colonial buildings disappeared. Whole districts were rebuilt. Between 1904 and 1905, the 108-foot (33-m) wide Avenida Central, later renamed Avenida Rio Branco, was built through the city's older, narrow streets. Two tunnel connections with the south zone were completed in 1892 and 1904 and the first skyscraper was built in 1925. The cog railroad to Corcovado Mountain was inaugurated in 1884, and the cable car up Sugarloaf Mountain was operational in 1912. Hills were leveled and the earth was used to

▲ Dom Pedro II, Emperor of Brazil from 1840–1889, took steps to industrialize and modernize the country.

"Ouvidor Street possesses the best stores in the city and also the most frequented of the inevitable cafes...here may be seen the well-groomed Brazilian merchant with his lady friends attired in the latest creations from Paris, sitting side by side with an estate owner from the interior, dressed in a loose-fitting coat and white trousers [pants]..."

—Charles Domville-Fife, twentieth-century explorer and journalist

▲ *This late nineteenth-century photograph shows the cog railroad, inaugurated in 1884, leading up to the Corcovado Mountain peak.*

reclaim land in the bay, including the Santos Dumont Airport site and the six-lane highway skirting Copacabana Beach.

Growing Population

Between 1941 and 1944, another major access route, Avenida President Vargas, was built through the city center. The influx of people continued. The shortage of housing became acute, and high-rise apartment buildings sprang up in Copacabana. Those who could not afford decent housing flocked to the favelas.

Brasília

On April 21, 1960, President Juscelino Kubitschek inaugurated the new capital of Brasília in the empty wilderness of central

▲ *The cable car to the top of Sugarloaf Mountain starts close to the spot where Rio was founded, a small peninsula at the entrance of Guanabara Bay.*

Brazil. The time had come to replace Rio, with its overcrowding and communication problems, with a new and modern capital city. Rio never really recovered from the shock. Though it remains one of the world's favorite tourist spots, drugs and violence have been a big problem here for a long time. The UN Earth Summit was held in Rio in 1992, and the authorities promised to clean up the streets and improve housing conditions, particularly in the favelas. There are also more plans to promote tourism.

The Hollywood Connection

The early 1920s to the late 1950s have been described as Rio's "Golden Age." The city was a romantic, exotic destination for Hollywood movie stars and international high society. They came to play in the city's glamorous casinos and nightclubs. Rio was featured in the movie Flying Down to Rio, *in which the actors Fred Astaire and Ginger Rogers starred together for the first time. The famous Brazilian singer Carmen Miranda also starred in many Hollywood musicals in the 1940s. She was renowned for her fabulous costumes and headdress piled high with fruit. There is a museum in Rio dedicated to her.*

CHAPTER 2

People of Rio

Rio's population was more than half a million at the beginning of the twentieth century. Within twenty years, it had doubled. By 1940, it had reached almost 2 million, and in the mid-1970s, it reached about 5 million.

Immigrants

In the early years of the twentieth century, many immigrants arrived from Europe, especially from Portugal, Spain, and Italy. Then, in the 1930s, the agricultural economy of Brazil was hit badly. Tens of thousands of people, especially from the drought-ridden northeast, left their homes and headed south (to Rio and São Paulo, a city to the south) hoping for a better life. By 1970, about 45 percent of the people living in Rio had not been born there.

Class and Race

Most Cariocas are of mixed origins: black African and European descent or *mestizos* of European and Native American descent. The cultural effect of black Africans in Rio has been obvious since they first arrived in the seventeenth century. They have shaped the music, food, and fashions of the city and of much of coastal eastern Brazil. Rio's famous annual Carnival has its origins in

◄ *This Carioca family lives in one of the many favelas where millions of Rio's poor citizens live.*

African lore, and many Cariocas practice African spiritual religions. White immigrants or people of European descent have had less impact, though today they often hold the most important jobs. They live mainly in the more affluent suburbs, such as Ipanema, Leblon, and Barra da Tijuca. There are differences in class and race in Rio, but the most obvious distinction is the huge gap between rich and poor. While the rich live in luxurious apartments, attended by maids and gardeners, and which have swimming pools and tennis courts, the poor live in miserable conditions with barely enough to eat. Whether living in a favela or a wealthy suburb, however, the most important unit for Cariocas is their family. In many households, several generations still live together.

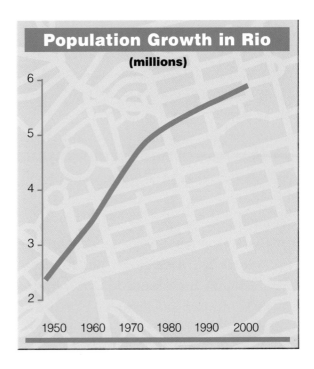

Population Growth in Rio
(millions)

Jogo do Bicho

Jogo do Bicho is part of Carioca life. It is an illegal game of gambling that started about a century ago, when a zoo owner, Baron de Drummond, needed to raise money for the upkeep of his animals. The gamble was to guess which of twenty-five pictures of animals he had placed in a sealed bag. The game caught on and was later refined by adding more numbers and animals. By the mid-1970s, thirty thousand people in Rio were thought to be involved in running the game, and the daily turnover was close to 3.3 million reais (about one million U.S. dollars). It is now played all over Brazil.

Roman Catholics

The Portuguese brought Christianity to Brazil, and most Cariocas are Roman Catholics. Baptism, confirmation, and marriage in church are still an essential part of family life. Churches in Rio are open during the day for Mass and other services. The Metropolitan Cathedral, completed in 1976, is big enough to hold twenty thousand people.

"Cariocas of every class thrive on crowds, the pulse of the samba, the restless movimento and late nights of the city. 'The Carioca night' the saying goes, 'has more than twelve hours.'"

—Douglas Botting, twentieth-century travel writer.

Christmas and Easter are public holidays. Other special days include St. Francis of Assisi day, October 4, when animals are taken to certain churches to be blessed. During Our Lady of Copacabana week, the patron saint of Copacabana, Nossa Senhora de Copacabana, is honored with religious ceremonies and a candlelight procession.

Christians
There are also churches of other Christian denominations, including the Anglican Christ Church, first founded in 1819 for the British Protestant immigrants. Evangelical churches are relatively new but are becoming increasingly popular.

Alternative Religions
A great many Cariocas from all ethnic, social, and economic backgrounds belong to African spiritual religions. The main religions are Candomblé, Kardecism, and Umbanda, and their central belief is that people can communicate with spirits. These date back to the time when Yoruba slaves arrived from West Africa. Slaves were forbidden from practicing their religion but managed to deceive their European masters by disguising their own gods, called *Orixás*, within the Catholic religion.

In ceremonies, they dance and sing to the beat of drums, offer gifts, and a medium (always male) induces a spirit to appear. Once possessed, the medium goes into a trance, takes on the character of the spirit and conveys the spirit's thoughts and wishes

"Eh! Rio...
Pretends that nothing's serious, not a bit
Yet cherishes at heart religious awe,
A sacred mysticism all-embracing
Witchcraft black or white, Ogum [god
of war] and Yemanjá"

—From *Portrait of a City*, by Carlos Drummond de Andrade, a twentieth-century poet.

to his followers. Spirits are called on to resolve many kinds of problems or to heal the sick. There are also dark, evil, and much-feared spirits.

New Year's Eve
Every New Year's Eve, followers of Umbanda celebrate the Festival of Yemanjá, goddess of the sea, on Copacabana Beach. Men and women, many dressed in white, light candles and bonfires and make small offerings of food and beverages. They chant and twirl to the beat of drums. At exactly midnight, they go to the water's edge and send white flowers and small decorated boats full of candles and gifts out to sea in her honor.

Food
In Rio, you can eat food from all the many regions of Brazil. Dishes from the northeast Bahia region, influenced by African traditions, contain coconut milk, dende oil (Brazilian palm oil), shrimp, and a large variety of fish. These are often turned into soups and stews.

Dishes from southern Brazil, where there are large cattle ranches, often include large quantities of beef.

Dining Out

At restaurants called *churrascarias*, waiters ask what kind of meat you would like and carve it at your table. You can eat as much as you like for the same price, and there is a red and green light system to indicate when you

▼ *New Year's Eve offerings are made to Yemanjá, goddess of the sea, on Copacabana Beach.*

Christ the Redeemer

Perched atop of Corcovado Mountain, Rio's statue of Christ the Redeemer is considered one of the modern wonders of the world. It is 98 feet (30 m) high and weighs 1,145 tons (1,039 metric tons). The idea of a statue was conceived in 1921 to celebrate the centennial of Brazil's independence the following year. Designed and created by Heitor de Silva Costa and Polish sculptor Paul Landowski, the statue was erected on October 12, 1931.

▲ *Many Cariocas enjoy a* rodizio, *a meal of various types of meat that are sliced at the table.*

have had enough. Vegetables are served separately. Restaurants where you serve yourself from a buffet and pay according to the weight of your plate are also very popular. Fast-food restaurants have opened in almost every part of Rio in recent years and are popular with city workers for quick lunches or snacks and with families for meals in the evenings. A *botequin*, or small bar-restaurant, is also a feature of life for many younger middle-income Cariocas, especially those working in the arts and media. The botequins usually have a "bohemian," or unconventional, atmosphere.

Most people who can afford to dine out often eat standing up at the counter of a diner or snack bar where they may enjoy

a *salgadinho* (a salty appetizer) with a *chope*, or *chopp* (draft light beer), or *guarana* (a type of soda).

Feijoada

The basic foods for most Brazilians are black beans and rice, sometimes eaten with chicken or meat. The main meal of the day is lunch, and on Saturdays, this means eating *feijoada*, regarded by many as Brazil's national dish. It takes many hours to prepare feijoada and most of the afternoon to eat it. Black beans are cooked with several kinds of meat: jerked beef, smoked

▲ *A woman serves meat, beans, rice, and kale for a feijoada, along with many other local dishes.*

sausage, smoked hog's tongue, and salt pork. The dish is served with rice, chopped kale, slices of orange, and *farofa*, which is ground cassava flour mixed with egg or spices and herbs.

Fruit Juice

Brazil produces a huge variety of fruit. In addition to bananas, apples, and plums, there are less well-known fruits such as mangoes, papayas, guavas, custard apples, *maracujas* (passion fruit), and *amoras* (a raspberry that looks like a strawberry). Almost all fruits are made into delicious fruit juices and ice creams. Coffee is a very popular beverage in Brazil. Drunk at any time during the day, it is served very strong and very sweet, in small cups known as *cafezinhos*.

Cariocas

A very quick and easy snack to make is "Cariocas." All you have to do is spread a sharp cheese onto small slices of bread. Place a thin piece of banana on top of each slice and pop them into an oven until the cheese melts.

CHAPTER 3

Living in Rio

Rio can be exotic and exciting. The bars, clubs, and music can lend atmosphere even in the dullest days of winter. However, many of its wealthier inhabitants leave on the weekends, often driving to their *sitios* (country homes). Many Cariocas now say that the violence of the city leaves them stressed, and they have to watch where they walk, even in daytime.

Colonial Buildings

One of the few places left in Rio with colonial and nineteenth-century buildings is the hilly suburb of Santa Teresa, to the southwest of the city center. The convent in Santa Teresa, built about 1750, is still used by Carmelite nuns, and among the narrow, curving, tree-lined streets are some old mansions, most of which have been turned into museums. The hills have a cooling effect on the weather and the area attracts wealthy Cariocas and foreigners. Today, many of the houses are occupied by artists, intellectuals, and craftspeople.

Housing

Most Cariocas live either in an apartment building or a favela. As the population grew in the twentieth century, the demand

◄ Hundreds of simple homes made of brick, sheet iron, and wood are crammed together in this hillside favela in Rio.

for housing forced Rio to expand upward. This was most obvious in Copacabana. Running parallel to the 3-mile (5-km) long beach are row upon row of tall apartment buildings. The population density of Rio is still one of the highest in the world. Gradually, as people have moved down the coast, more and more apartment buildings have appeared. Many have swimming pools, tennis courts, and other modern facilities and are designed mainly for the wealthier Cariocas.

Favelas

Some working-class Cariocas have substantial brick houses in the northern suburbs, but many, together with Rio's poor citizens, live in favelas. The people of the favelas, called *favelados*, number more than 1.2 million. Some of these shantytowns are

▲ *The statue of Christ the Redeemer looks down from the heights of Corcovado Mountain on the church of Nossa Senhora da Glória do Outeiro.*

better than others; the worst are built using wooden planks and sheet iron and without running water, lights, or sanitation. Roads are unpaved and unlit, and there is no trash collection or sewer system. Most homes consist of two rooms at ground level, with others being added above as money and time permit. The favelados build their own homes or work together on several houses. Furniture is simple. Beds, tables, and chairs are often homemade or are the work of a local carpenter. Water is scarce for many homes and has to be carried from a community pump. Electricity is usually pirated from the nearest pole. Yet somehow, even in such adversity, the community spirit

Famous Architects

Lucio Costa (1902–1998) and Oscar Niemeyer (1907–) are world famous as the designer and architect, respectively, of the new capital of Brasília. Both studied in Rio and first worked together on the Ministry of Education building (1936–1946), which has been described as the first truly modern building in South America. They also worked together on the Baixada de Jacarepaguá project, built in the swamps near Barra da Tijuca in the 1970s. The project now houses 3.5 million people.

is dominant. Many Cariocas enjoy watching television together, with a special interest for national sporting events and the string of nightly soap operas, or *novelas*.

Shopping

Shopping is a favorite pastime in Rio. Most Cariocas love to follow the latest fashion and spend 7 percent of their gross income on clothing. The most popular places to shop

▼ *Shoppers browse in one of Rio's many modern malls. Following the latest fashion is important to many Cariocas.*

▶ *A streetside herbalist uses a wooden pestle and mortar to make health-food drinks for passersby.*

are the city's shopping malls. Since 1981, the number of malls in Rio has jumped from two to thirty-two. Most are in the suburbs. Two of the newest are Carioca Shopping in a northern district and Center Shopping in the Jacarepaguá suburbs in the west.

A typical mall has large stores with domestic and international brand names and small boutiques that often belong to individual traders selling clothing, jewelry, or things for the home. Shoe manufacturing is a big industry in Brazil, so there are many shoe stores. Brazilians are also eager purchasers of cell phones, computers, and stereo equipment. Some shopping malls have computers for Internet and e-mail use, and there are always people standing in line to pay to use them. Most malls have snack bars, ice cream parlors, and restaurants, but Carioca Shopping also has an eight-screen movie theater, and another mall, Lojas Americanas, has a small amusement park. The greatest advantage of the malls is that they are safe. Rio is a dangerous city for a shopper carrying bags and money. There are many muggings and robberies. The malls employ a large number of security guards, and there are video cameras everywhere.

Markets

Across the city there are small stores and supermarkets, and the favelas have their own small stores. Stores may be owned by

Herbal Medicines

Every city in South America has plenty of drugstores, and Rio is no different. However, many people still prefer to use traditional herbal medicines. These are sometimes sold on the street, where herbs are neatly laid out on the sidewalk with notices indicating what they will treat or cure. The seller sits with a huge pestle and mortar (above), which he or she uses to prepare mixtures as they are requested.

families. Supermarkets are usually part of a chain. They sell all the normal household materials, fruits and vegetables, meat, alcohol and everything you would find in a Western supermarket. Many Cariocas, however, prefer to go to open-air markets because the prices are often lower, and there are several excellent markets that sell fresh-cut flowers, fruits, vegetables, meats, and cheeses. Markets are held on different days of the week in different suburbs. There are also household goods markets in various parts of the city. Perhaps Rio's best-known permanent market is the Cobal in Botafogo. Half of the area is used to sell vegetables and fruits and the other half is filled with bars and restaurants, some with live music.

A Bit of Everything

Copacabana and other places in the south zone have elegant fashion and tourist shops, including gem and jewelry stores selling precious and semiprecious stones such as emeralds, topaz, and amethyst, which are mined in other parts of Brazil. Tourists are also attracted to the art, antiques, and handicraft markets in Ipanema.

Education

The Brazilian education system includes both public and private institutions, ranging from kindergarten to college and post-graduate levels. Free public education is available at all levels. Church-run schools are also available.

Education is compulsory for children seven to fourteen years of age, but many children do not attend school. The children of favela families are often too poor to afford transportation to school and instead have to find whatever work they can to earn money for their families. Charities fund a few places where orphaned and street

children can take classes and get a meal. Despite the problems, Rio has one of the highest literacy rates in Brazil, with about 90 percent of the population over the age of ten able to read and write.

School Shifts

The academic year runs from February to November, with breaks for summer and Easter. Public schools tend to run in two shifts, with classes for some children in the morning and for others in the afternoon. Often, these schools do not have enough teachers or teaching materials. The curriculum is much the same as in schools in the United States or Europe and includes science, languages, arts, South American and world history, geography, and physical education.

Private Education

With bigger budgets, private schools can afford to offer a better level of education. Most of these private schools are found in the south zone of the city. They include the American and British schools where children are taught in English. Children in most private schools wear a uniform of a white T-shirt with the school's logo emblazoned on it with jeans or a skirt.

College

Rio also has many public and private colleges. The oldest public college in the city, the federal University of Rio de Janeiro, was established in 1920. Other

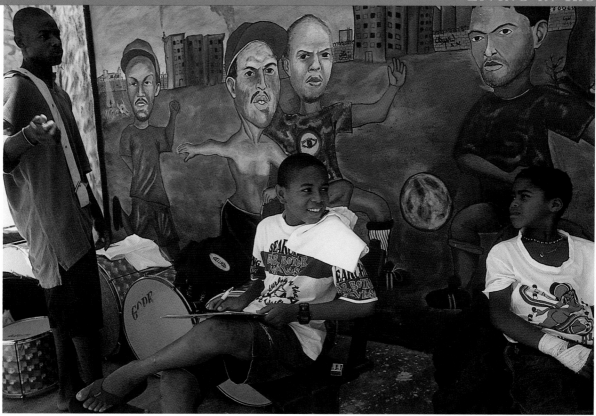

▲ Many favela children enjoy projects designed to encourage them to develop their talents in music and dance.

colleges include the University of Rio de Janeiro, founded in 1969, and the Pontifical Catholic University.

Culture

Even though it is no longer the capital city, Rio remains the cultural center of Brazil. It is the home of the National Library and has many fine museums. These include the National Museum, the Museum of Modern Art, the National Fine Arts Museum, and the National Historical Museum. The Municipal Theater, built in 1905, is the home of Rio's ballet and opera companies.

Central Station

Central Station, directed by Walther Salles, is a landmark in Brazilian movie history. It won a Golden Globe Award for best foreign language film in 1998. The movie is about the relationship between a middle-aged woman, Dora, and a young orphan boy, Josue, who meet at Rio's main railroad station. Dora spends her days writing letters for many of the illiterate travelers who pass through the station, often taking their money and never mailing the envelopes. Now, two typists, inspired by the movie, work on computers in a small office in the actual railroad terminal in Rio. They handle three to four letters a day and will produce résumés for job seekers. The service is free for illiterate clients.

▶ *Rio de Janeiro is one of the most polluted cities in the world. This graph shows suspended particles (smoke, soot, dust, and liquid droplets that are in the air) and sulfur dioxide (the air pollutant formed when fossil fuels containing sulfur are burned). The World Health Organization standards for acceptable air quality are 90 micrograms per cubic meter (mg/m^3) for total suspended particles and 50 mg/m^3 for sulfur dioxide.*

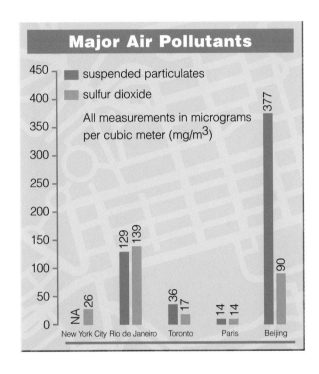

Major Air Pollutants

- suspended particulates
- sulfur dioxide

All measurements in micrograms per cubic meter (mg/m^3)

New York City: NA, 26
Rio de Janeiro: 129, 139
Toronto: 36, 17
Paris: 14, 14
Beijing: 377, 90

Pollution

Heavy traffic and industry are causing severe pollution in Rio, especially in the northern suburbs. The Clean Air Initiative (a project promoted by municipalities of metropolitan Rio, the State Foundation for Engineering and Environment, the Federal University of Rio de Janeiro, and the Ministry of Environment) is particularly aimed at this problem and hopes to improve the air quality and reduce pollution. Rio's geographical position does not help: incoming winds across the bay are blocked by the mountain ranges behind the city, so the pollution cannot be dispersed easily.

Sewer Systems

Some of the main beaches, including Copacabana, are also polluted and not considered safe for bathing. This is due to Rio's inadequate sewer systems and the domestic and industrial waste that has been pumped directly out into the ocean. Lagoons and lakes, once full of fish and birds, are now severely polluted. In 1990,

local fishers caught 800 tons (725 metric tons) of shrimp there. In 1999, they caught none. The Rio state and city governments have joined together to invest more than 200 million U.S. dollars into a new sewage-treatment plant.

Crime

Crime is also a huge problem in Rio. Street muggings and robberies are commonplace throughout the city. In 1994, a particularly bad year, the city had one of the worst murder rates in the world. Much of the violence stems from the drug trade and rival favela gangs, helped along by a corrupt police force. The fact that the favelas are generally surrounded by wealthy suburbs, which are a temptation and easily accessible, also pushes crime rates up.

City of God

Cidade de Deus, or City of God, is one of Rio's most notorious favelas. The city began in the 1960s as a government project of simple brick houses set out in rows with earthen streets, in Jacarepaguá, in southwest Rio. The project was to move people from the (now prosperous) areas of Lagoa and Leblon to make way for apartment buildings. Organized crime and drugs took a foothold in the City of God, and by the beginning of the 1980s, it became one of the most dangerous places in Rio. Today, about 190,000 people live there and the laws within the favela are made by teenage drug barons and gang leaders. There are an estimated 120 murders a year. City of God is also the title of a recent, popular Brazilian movie telling the story of two boys brought up against a background of violence and drugs.

Health Care

Rio has many doctors and hospitals. Most are found in the affluent south zone, but there is a system of public hospitals and clinics that provide at least some free health care even to the city's poorest residents. In 2002, Rio was hit by an epidemic of dengue fever, a disease that is transmitted by mosquitoes. In January and February of that year alone, twenty-four people died and over fifty thousand were infected with the disease.

◀ In recent years, the army has been called in to help control drug gangs operating in the streets of Rio.

CHAPTER 4

Rio at Work

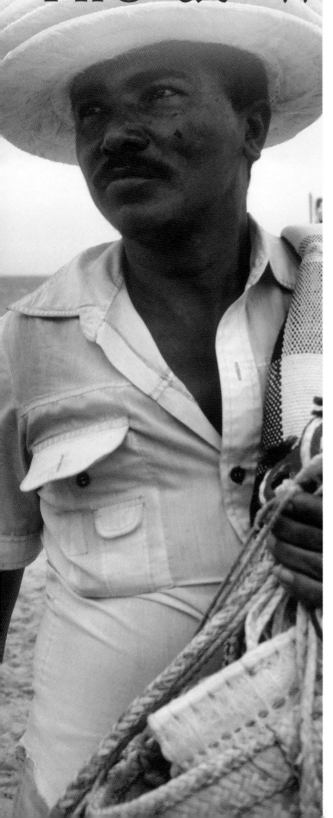

Rio is the second-largest manufacturing center in Brazil (after São Paulo). Many Cariocas are employed in factories that produce clothing and footwear, processed food, beverages, and pharmaceuticals. Many people are also employed in the printing, publishing, glassworking, and shipbuilding industries. Recently, an electronics and computer sector has opened up. Most of the factories are in the north and west of the city. Rio is also at the center of Brazil's oil industry. Guanabara Bay is a natural harbor and storage depot for the gigantic oil platforms used offshore in the Atlantic. Petrobras, the Brazilian oil company, has a refinery at Duque de Caxias in metropolitan Rio. Offshore fields contain more than 80 percent of the country's oil reserves.

Fast Moving

The administrative offices of many of Brazil's large corporations are in Rio, and the city is still Brazil's second most important financial center (after São Paulo), with a stock market and a large number of banks. The offices of many of these companies are found in the city center. Like most major cities, rush hours at about 9:00 A.M.

◄ *The beaches of Rio are the perfect place for traders to sell goods such as straw hats, towels, and beverages.*

and 5:00 P.M. bring the city's traffic to a virtual standstill.

Big Businesses

Corporations in Rio include the Rio Doce Valley Company, a state mining enterprise, Exxon, Shell, and Gillette, all multinational corporations, and Banco Nacional de Desenvolvimento Econômico e Social (BNDES), the country's largest investment bank. Offices are modern and well equipped and use the most sophisticated information technology systems available.

▼ *Rio's Sugarloaf Mountain (left, in background) can be seen across the sprawling suburb of Niterói, on the eastern side of Guanabara Bay.*

Niterói

The city of Niterói is on the eastern side of Guanabara Bay. Today, it is part of metropolitan Rio and is a residential suburb. Niterói is also the site of Brazil's chief shipbuilding and ship-repair yards. It is connected to Rio by the 9-mile (14-km) President Costa e Silva Bridge, one of the longest bridges in Brazil. Every day, some 200,000 commuters cross the bridge or travel by ferry to and from work.

The television and publishing empire of Roberto Marinho is also based in Rio. It is the world's fourth-largest television network after NBC, ABC, and CBS.

Unemployment

Cariocas who have no regular employment often work on the streets and most need more than one job to survive. Some become street traders selling food, beverages, or cigarettes. Others head to the beaches where they sell goods such as hats, towels, and refreshing beverages. Cariocas sometimes find temporary work on building sites or in markets. A few of the luckier ones may be able to get a license and share a car to run as a taxi service.

Child Workers

Children of the poorest Cariocas also find themselves in the streets trying to earn money. They clean cars and car windows, look after cars in parking lots, or sell newspapers or chewing gum at traffic lights. They may also clean shoes or run errands, anything that will earn them some money.

Tourism

Many people in Rio are involved in the tourist industry. Rio is famous worldwide, and thousands of visitors arrive by air, sea, train, bus, and car from neighboring Latin American countries and from overseas. There are about 2 million visitors each year, boosting the demand for new hotels, which is good for Rio's construction industry. The city also has hundreds of restaurants that provide work for chefs and waiters.

Transportation

Cariocas use public buses more than any other form of transportation. Buses are cheap and connect with every part of the city, but they are very crowded and move slowly in the congested streets. There are plenty of bus stops in the city center, with details of where and what time buses run. On the outskirts of the city, where there are few or no bus stops, people flag down buses as they pass, and if necessary, the bus will

◄ *A view up Avenida Delfim Moreira, of Leblon Beach, shows the peaks of Dois Irmãos, or "Two Brothers."*

The Bondinho

The last electric streetcar in Rio, known locally as the bondinho, *runs between Largo de Carioca and the suburb of Santa Teresa, passing over the top of the Arcos de Carioca (the Carioca Aqueduct). The first streetcar ran along the tracks on top of the arches on September 1, 1896. The streetcars got the nickname "bondes" from the share "bonds" used to finance them. Gradually, during the twentieth century, they were closed down as other forms of transportation proved quicker and more efficient.*

cross three lanes of traffic to pick them up. There are at least 430 bus routes run by municipal Rio authorities.

Taxis in Rio are identified by their red license plates with white figures, but some simply say "TAXI" on the windshield or roof. Traffic congestion was eased slightly when, in 1997, a new expressway, the Linha Amarela, was built. It has helped to lessen some of Rio's worst traffic jams.

Cars

It can be nerve-racking to drive in Rio. The locals drive fast and with confidence. Robberies from cars are quite frequent. Drivers tend to keep their doors locked and big, expensive cars often have tinted windows. Bus passengers also have to take great care because robbery is common there, too.

▼ *The last of Rio's streetcars, the bondinho, runs from the line's end station near Largo da Carioca to Santa Teresa and is often crowded with passengers sitting inside and hanging from the outside of the car.*

Petrópolis

Petrópolis is one of the cities in the metropolitan Rio de Janeiro area. Located in the Serra do Mar Mountains, it is a beautiful city full of flowers. The site, founded in 1843, was chosen by Emperor Dom Pedro II for his summer palace. Each year, the royal family spent six months there, and gradually the city developed. The addition of a railroad in 1854 made the journey to Rio much easier, and effectively, Petrópolis became the country's administrative capital for half of every year. Early in the twentieth century, it was the Brazilian president's official summer residence. Now, it is an industrial center, but it is also popular with tourists.

Trains

For a city of more than 14 million people, metropolitan Rio has a very small rail network, with only two lines. Opened in 1979, it covers about 22 miles (35 km). Line one is completely underground and runs from Copacabana to the city center, via Central Station, and then to Sáens Pena, the station nearest to Tijuca National Park. The Copacabana station, Cardeal Arcoverde, was opened in 1998. It took years of tunneling to complete because it is built 60 feet (18 m) below sea level, inside a mountain. It is connected to the street by eight escalators and three moving sidewalks. Line two is partly over ground and runs from the city center to the northwest districts. Another line is planned that will link the international airport with Barra da Tijuca, Rio's longest beach. A train service in the city, the SuperVia, connects to the *Metrô* (subway) system to carry passengers to suburban destinations.

Flight

Rio has two airports. The international airport is on the large Ilha de Governador (Governor Island) in Guanabara Bay. Antonio Carlos Jobim Airport (formerly known as Galeão), was renamed after the musician who wrote the famous song "Girl from Ipanema." Santos Dumont is the downtown airport, named after one of Brazil's first aviators. In the heart of the city center, the Santos Dumont Airport is built on reclaimed land opposite Sugarloaf Mountain. A shuttle service from Santos Dumont flies to São Paulo every thirty minutes.

Governing Rio

Because it served as the capital of Brazil until 1960, Rio was considered a federal district. The district stood in the state of Guanabara. After Brasília became the capital, the states of Guanabara and the federal district merged to become the state of Rio de Janeiro, with Rio as its capital.

Municipalities

Metropolitan Rio is made up of fourteen independent municipalities, including Rio itself; Nova Iguaçú and Duque de Caxias in the industrial north; Niterói; and Petrópolis,

an attractive city in the mountains about 43 miles (69 km) from downtown Rio. The people from each municipality are able to elect their own mayor and council, who are responsible for overseeing elementary education, basic health care, trash collection, and maintenance of the streets and parks in their area. Rio elects its *prefeito*, or mayor, for a four-year term, and he or she can be re-elected for one further term. The Municipal Chamber's members are elected from the municipalities of metropolitan Rio.

▲ *Guanabara Palace, the one-time presidential palace, is now the office of the governor of the state of Rio de Janeiro.*

Mayors

Cesar Maia was mayor of Rio from 1993 to 1996 and was re-elected in 2001. He has been eager to promote new development in a derelict, run-down area of the city's port. The plan, known as the Guggenheim Museum Rio de Janeiro, has been developed with the Guggenheim Museum in New York. It would include a museum, galleries, restaurants, and stores. Much of the museum would be built under water. The cost of about 250 million U.S. dollars could be a problem, however. Mayor Maia's supporters argue that the building would bring Rio tremendous prestige, establish a first-class museum in South America, bring new jobs, and attract thousands of tourists. Opponents of the plan say that, given the level of poverty in the city, the money should be spent to provide hospitals and schools, look after the children who live on the streets, and provide running water to the 20 percent of the population who do not have it.

CHAPTER 5

Rio at Play

Originally a Christian pre-Lenten festival, Carnival in Rio is an amazing spectacle. It is held on the weekend before Shrove Tuesday (in either February or March). At the heart of Carnival are the samba schools, which parade in the Sambódromo, a permanent site designed by Oscar Niemeyer that has seating space for sixty thousand people . This site also has an avenue about 2,300 feet (700 m) long that is lined with stands, seating, bars, and media areas. The parades begin at 7:00 P.M. and last throughout the night. Mangueira, Beja Flor, and Mocidade are some of the best-known schools. Each school has an average of four thousand dancers and up to thirty floats. The schools have to choose a theme, compose their own music, and design costumes and floats to fit their theme. This takes many months and much of the work is done in the poorer districts. The costumes are a fantastic riot of color in chiffons, silks, satins, sequins, beads, and feathers.

Competitive Carnival

Dancers are divided into groups, or "wings," and each is costumed differently. One wing is made up of the *bateria*, or percussion musicians. With tambourines, rattles, and drums, they maintain a reverberating beat

◀ *A dancer in a costume typical of northeast Brazil joins in a street parade during Rio's annual Carnival.*

that keeps the dancers and spectators constantly on the move. This is important because the samba school must complete the length of the Sambódromo within a specified time. Carnival is, in fact, a very serious competition. Each school is judged on the performance of its dancers, costume designs, and music. There is an eventual winner, who can expect to receive good recording contracts for the music with potentially very profitable sales. During Carnival week, neighborhoods, or *blocos*, in the city also have their own local parades in which anyone can join, and there are many parties and balls.

▲ *A Carnival float, adorned with two immense gilded lions, passes down the main avenue of the Sambódromo.*

Museums

Outside of Carnival week, Rio has many museums and old palaces set in beautiful parks where Cariocas can go to relax, play soccer, or have picnics. Boa Vista is a popular park to visit and is crowded on weekends. It was the residence of the imperial family in the nineteenth century. Other favorite outings include trips to the National Observatory and to the zoo with its colorful tropical birds. Among the many

"Of all the riches manifested in the Brazilian Carnival, none comes close to the Carioca Carnival in Rio de Janeiro, the model of which has become imprinted on the entire nation due to the Samba Schools."

—Lelia Gonzales,
Brazilian folklore specialist and anthropologist.

museums, the new Modern Art Museum is a spectacular building, while the Museum of Naïve Art, founded in 1995, has a fascinating collection. It displays the work of naïve painters — untrained artists who use vibrant colors and generally paint daily scenes, folk festivals, and landscapes.

Roberto Burle Marx

Landscape designer and artist Roberto Burle Marx (1909–1994), was famous for the gardens he designed in the city of Brasília. However, his home and the site of his estate, Barra de Guaratiba, are near Rio. The estate contains 3,500 species of plants, mostly Brazilian, and is now open to the public. In the 1960s, he created the Flamengo Park on land reclaimed from the ocean. It contains sports fields, a miniature village, a theater for children, bandstands, and areas for dancing.

Music

Wealthier Cariocas have their own private clubs to go to, but for the majority of Cariocas, the amount of choice for recreation depends on the suburb they live in. Music festivals or presentations by Brazilian and international artists are held in open arenas, such as the Canecao, beside Botafogo Bay, or on specially constructed stages on a beach.

Soccer

All Brazilians are passionate about *futebol*, or soccer, and Cariocas are no exception. For the young and poor, becoming a famous soccer professional is one of the few legal ways of escaping poverty and the favelas.

◄ *Sugarloaf Mountain overlooks the exclusive district of Urca and Botafogo Bay, one of Rio's most traditional neighborhoods.*

▲ *Vasco da Gama and Flamengo, two of Rio's famous soccer clubs, play in a fiercely competitive game held in the Maracanã stadium.*

Youngsters play soccer everywhere — in the street, backyards, parks, and on the beaches, where there are often well-organized training sessions and competitions. Adults, too, spend their breaks from work in friendly matches and are often found on the beaches late at night kicking a ball around.

The Maracanã stadium was built in 1950 for the World Cup games, and the final match that year, between Brazil and Uruguay, drew a crowd of almost 200,000, the largest number of spectators on record anywhere. The Maracanã is one of the world's largest stadiums, but for many years now, it has been in decline. Today, only about 80,000 spectators are allowed in at any one time because parts of the building are unsafe. Nonetheless, a match held there is a fantastic occasion, with samba bands, fireworks, and good-natured, if raucous, supporters.

Racing

Brazil has produced some of the world's most famous grand prix racing drivers, including Nelson Piquet (from Rio) and Ayrton Senna. The Brazilian Grand Prix

Pan American Games

In 2007, Rio will host the Pan American Games. The games started in 1951 and take place every four years. Competitors come from North, Central, and South America and the Caribbean islands. The Pan American Games are similar to the Olympic Games, with most sports represented. Rio has also submitted its name in the hopes that it will be chosen to host the Olympic Games of 2012.

is held, on alternate years, in Rio and in São Paulo. The Rio track, the Autódromo, is in Rio's Jacarepaguá district in the south zone.

Other Sports

Rio has sports facilities and clubs of every kind and many gyms. Sports such as golf, tennis, horseback riding, and sailing are exclusively for more wealthy Cariocas. A favorite sailing venue is the Lagoa Rodrigo de Freitas, a lagoon located between Ipanema and the shore of Rio. Those who take up hang gliding, parachuting, and paragliding, are rewarded with some of the best views of Rio and its beaches.

Sun Worshiping

Cariocas love their beaches, which is not at all surprising as Rio has some of the most beautiful beaches in South America. Copacabana and Ipanema are always crowded. The beaches are not just for sunbathing, though there are plenty who do sunbathe. The beaches are used for many activities — some of Brazil's Olympic teams train on the beaches. Visitors have to take care, however, as they can be targeted by thieves, despite the security cameras used by some hotels to monitor their beaches.

▼ *Crowds of Cariocas enjoy one of Rio's favorite pastimes — basking in the sun on the city's beaches.*

▲ *Surfing is a popular sport in Rio all year round. The best waves are found during the winter months, from June to August.*

Days Out

The two most popular excursions in Rio are the ride up Sugarloaf Mountain by cable car and a visit to the statue of Christ the Redeemer. The cable car ride starts close to the spot where Rio was founded. An exhibition at the cable car station shows photographs of the first wooden streetcars that used to carry just twenty-three passengers. The track for the first stage, to Urca, was laid in 1912. Today's cars carry more than one hundred passengers. At the top of Urca and Sugarloaf Mountain are restaurants and stores, and fantastic views of Rio, its beaches, Guanabara Bay, the statue of Christ, and Niterói. For those with the energy, it is also possible to climb Sugarloaf Mountain. The journey to the statue of Christ can be done by road or by the railroad opened in 1884 by Emperor Dom Pedro II. From the train's end station, there is a climb of over two hundred steps to the statue, where the view is magnificent.

Tijuca National Park

Coffee was first planted in Rio in 1760 in the forested Tijuca Mountains. The rain forest was soon cut down to make way for coffee plantations, and, on the lower slopes, sugar plantations. In 1861, the Emperor Dom Pedro II decided to reforest the whole area, and it was later turned into a national park. There are now many species of trees and plants in the park and a good variety of wildlife. A paved road winds to the highest point at more than 3,250 feet (1,000 m) from which there is a fine view of Rio and Guanabara Bay.

CHAPTER 6

Looking Forward

In 1992, Rio hosted the United Nations (UN) Earth Summit, where the state of the planet and the extensive poverty in certain parts of the world were discussed. Like many countries, Brazil agreed to do more to help its poor citizens and improve the quality of the environment. Everyone recognizes that Rio's favelas pose a massive problem for the city. They are not good for the people who live in them, and they are not good for the image of Rio.

Housing Projects

In the 1960s, the authorities tried to move some favelados to better housing on the outskirts of Rio, but the plan failed because the people were too far from their place of work. The municipal government introduced a new proposal in 1993 to improve the favelas and integrate them into surrounding neighborhoods. The project is called *Favela-bairro*, which means "from favela to residential neighborhood." The plan involves bringing to the favelas essential amenities such as electricity, water, a sewer system, child care centers, and paved streets. It also means replacing the makeshift homes with better forms of housing, and where possible, building

◀ *Children gather beneath a Golden Tree of Life, symbolizing the future of Earth, at the UN Earth Summit held in Rio in 1992.*

community centers and health clinics. The cost of converting each house is about $2,500 in U.S. dollars, and since 1995, the government, aided by the Inter-American Development Bank (IDB), established in 1959 to help social and economic development in Latin America, has invested about 600 million U.S. dollars in the project. Another aspect of the plan is to encourage reforestation on the hills to help prevent landslides during heavy rains.

Already, some favelas have benefited from the plan. In the La Grota favela, where the work has been going on for six years, houses have now been connected to Rio's electricity and sewer systems. Almost all of the old wooden homes have been replaced by small concrete and brick houses, although many still have no windows. There is a child-care center, a soccer field, and a small playground. Perhaps the greatest joy for the favelados is that, for the first time, they now live on a paved street

▲ *The Tijuca National Park of Atlantic rain forest covers many of the hills and valleys near Rio.*

that has a name and in a house that has a number. This not only means they have a proper address, but now according to new legislation, they own the house and the land on which they live.

Simpatico

Rio is well known for its beauty and lively culture and, by contrast, for its unhealthy favelas and high rate of crime. Despite Rio's problems, in June 2003, following a six-year study by psychologists at California State University, Rio was pronounced the friendliest city in the world. In commenting on the report, the *New Scientist*, a London-based magazine, wrote that it all comes down to the Cariocas' reputation for being *simpatico*, or friendly and open. Most visitors to this exciting and welcoming world-class city would readily agree.

Time Line

January 1, 1502 Portuguese explorers arrive in what is now Rio de Janeiro.

1555 French settlers establish a base, called Antarctic France, on an island in middle of Guanabara Bay.

1560 Portuguese Governor Mem de Sá leads an expedition against the French.

1567 São Sebastião de Rio de Janeiro is founded by the Portuguese.

1624 The Church of Nossa Senhora do Cabeça is built.

1750 Arcos de Carioca is completed.

1750 The Convent of Santa Teresa is built.

1760s The first coffee is planted in the Tijuca Mountains.

1763 Rio replaces Salvador as capital of Brazil.

1807 Napoleon threatens to depose the Portuguese monarchy—Prince Regent Dom João and ten thousand of his courtiers leave for Brazil.

1808 Rio de Janeiro Botanical Gardens open.

1815 Dom João takes the title of King João IV of Brazil and Portugal.

1819 The Anglican Christ Church is founded.

1821 Dom João returns to Portugal, leaving his son Dom Pedro as regent.

1822 Dom Pedro proclaims Brazil's independence and becomes emperor.

1831 Dom Pedro I abdicates in favor of his son the future Dom Pedro II.

1843 Petrópolis is founded.

1861 Tijuca is reforested.

1884 A cog railroad to the Corcovado Mountain peak is opened by Dom Pedro II.

1888 Golden Law is passed, freeing all slaves.

1889 Royal family is banished from Brazil.

1904–05 The Avenida Central is built.

1905 The Municipal Theater is built.

1912 The cable car to Sugarloaf Mountain is inaugurated.

1920 Federal University is established.

1925 Rio's first skyscraper is built.

1931 The statue of Christ the Redeemer is built atop Corcovado Mountain.

1950 The Maracanã Stadium is built for the soccer World Cup.

1960 Brasília replaces Rio as the capital of Brazil.

1960s Flamengo Park is created by Roberto Burle Marx.

1969 The University of Rio de Janeiro is founded.

1976 Metropolitan Cathedral is completed.

1979 The Metrô opens.

1995 The Museum of Naïve Art is founded.

1998 Opening of Copacabana station, Cardeal Arcoverde.

2007 Rio will serve as the host city for the Pan American games.

Glossary

aqueduct a large channel built to carry water from one place to another.

aristocracy class of people who by birth or wealth are considered by some to rank above the rest of the community.

Carioca a person who lives in Rio de Janeiro. Also the name of a Brazilian snack.

colony a settlement of people from one country in another land, or a land or region governed by another country.

commuter a person who travels regularly to and from work.

corporation a group, often very large, of people who together form a company.

corrupt dishonest in government or business.

environment surroundings, especially the natural world.

estuary the mouth of a large river.

evangelical relates to the preaching of the Christian Gospels.

favela shantytown areas of cities and towns in Brazil.

immigrant a person who moves to a new country and settles there.

mestizos people of mixed Native American and Spanish or Portuguese ancestries.

metropolitan of or relating to a large city.

middle class the section of society between the poor and the wealthy. Usually including businesspeople, professionals, and skilled workers.

municipality an area of a town or city with local self-government.

outcrop the part of a rock formation that can be seen on the surface of the ground.

pharmaceutical relating to the preparation, use, or sale of medicinal drugs.

pollution the poisoning of land, water, or air by human activity such as industry, transportation, or agriculture.

Protestant describes a Christian tradition of worship derived from those who broke away from the Catholic Church in Europe in the 1500s.

refinery an industrial site where substances such as oil or sugar are refined.

regent a person authorized to govern a kingdom in the absence of the monarch.

Roman Catholic describes a Christian tradition of worship headed by the Pope in Rome.

rural relating to or involving the countryside.

settler someone who settles in a new country or area, particularly one that has not been occupied before.

suburb a residential district on the edge of a city or large town.

viceroy an official who serves as an appointed representative of the royal family and who governs the colony in their name.

Further Information

Books

Day, Mick and Ben Box. *Rio de Janeiro Handbook: The Travel Guide (Footprint Handbooks)*. McGraw-Hill, 2001.

Ferro, Jennifer. *Brazilian Foods and Culture*. Rourke Press, 1999.

Galvin, Irene Flum. *Brazil: Many Voices, Many Faces*. Benchmark Books, 1996.

Gresko, Marcia S. *Letters Home from: Brazil (Letters Home from)*. Gale Group, 1999.

Kent, Deborah. *Rio de Janeiro (Cities of the World)*. Children's Press, 1996.

Richard, Christopher. *Brazil (Cultures of the World)*. Marshall Cavendish, 2002.

Web sites

www.lonelyplanet.com/destinations/south_america/rio_de_janeiro/
Take an armchair tour of the attractions, activities, and basic information of Rio De Janeiro.

http://www.interknowledge.com/brazil/rio/index.htm
A geographical web site containing general information about Brazil and Rio de Janeiro.

http://www.un.org/Pubs/CyberSchoolBus/habitat/profiles/rio.asp
A United Nations web site giving a city profile of Rio de Janeiro.

http://www.rio.rj.gov.br/riotur/en/pagina/?Canal=152
A web site that's packed with a variety of interesting facts about the land, people, and history of Rio De Janeiro as well as a wide variety of maps.

http://www.en.wikipedia.org/wiki/Rio_de_Janeiro
Learn more details about Rio De Janeiro's founding, location, and future by exploring the provided links.

www.timeforkids.com/TFK/specials/goplaces/0,12405,190791,00.html
Meet some Brazilian kids your age and learn what their lives are like.

Index

Page numbers in **bold** indicate pictures.